Evan Doyle

INTENTIONAL SMALL GROUPS

A Complete Guide For Leading a Small Group

Intentional Small Groups
A Complete Guide For Leading a Small Group

Copyright © 2017 Evan Doyle

All rights reserved under International and Pan-American Copyright Conventions

No part of this book may be reproduced or transmitted in any form or by any means, electronic, graphic, or mechanical, including photocopying, recording, or by any information storage and retrieval system, without the written permission of the copyright owner.

ISBN-13: 978-0-989-13952-6

Printed in the United States

Dedication

To those at CFM who willingly led the way in creating small groups at our church and helped teach me what small groups can be and do.

Why Did I Write This Guide?

A few years ago I was asked to oversee (start) the small group ministry at the church where I'm one of the pastors. After trying multiple different ways to do groups we finally settled on a few important principles that guide our groups rather than a method of doing them.

This book is a not a system or methodology for doing groups, it is a guide that is divided into six parts that are specific to small group leadership. After leading groups myself, having conversations with other leaders, and receiving feedback from those involved, a couple key things began to surface concerning group life. Christian community and spiritual growth are two sides to one coin. I believe that if we are intentional about being around Christian community, spiritual growth will inevitably take place. Another way of putting it would be, if we are serious about growing spiritually we have to be involved in Christian community.

Whether you lead a group around a common interest, share a bible study, meet with other married couples, have a prayer group, or gather in a home or a coffee shop the principles in this guide will equip you for leading a successful small group.

I named the book *Intentional Small Groups* because great groups do not happen by accident. They are formed and forged by leaders who lead with purpose and great intentionality. I hope this book helps you to do the same.

If at any point while you're reading this guide you have questions please feel free to contact me. You can reach me on Twitter (@EvanDoyletweets), or on my Facebook Page. If you prefer email you can reach me at evan@dailychristianhelp.com.

Why Are Small Groups Valuable?

Small Groups can play an important role in fulfilling the Great Commission to lead people to Jesus and into a deeper relationship with God.

Community is vital for believers. The church does not just exist within the four walls of a building, but inside our homes, neighborhoods, and communities.

Small groups should be an intentional effort to create opportunity for believers and non-believers to experience community and grow spiritually through bible study and connecting with others.

There are a number of benefits that small groups provide to the Body of Christ at large and obviously to the individual:

- Christian Friendship Inspires Christian Living

- Accountability Will Produce Sincerity

- Opens Opportunity to Invite the Lost

- Extends the Pastoral Reach of Leaders and Churches

- Connection Leaves Little Reason for Leaving

What Should Small Groups Do?

Small groups should empower the Body of Christ to build community and experience spiritual growth. Simply put, small groups can provide opportunity to grow, laugh, serve, and connect with others for God's glory.

Small groups vary in size, interest, place of meeting, type, etc. Ultimately, whether a group is having a Bible study, serving the community, or sharing a common interest, small groups should facilitate Christian community and spiritual growth.

Contents

1. Serving Is Leading — 1
2. Reliability Over Qualifications — 5
3. Priority And Practice Of Bible Study — 9
4. Using Your Time Wisely — 15
5. What Exercise Reminded Me About Spiritual Growth? — 19
6. Are You Responsible For The Spiritual Growth Of Others? — 23
7. How To Help Others Grow Spiritually — 27
8. How A Group Environment Can Facilitate Spiritual Growth — 31
9. Why Multiplication Matters — 33
10. Identifying Leadership Within Your Small Group — 37
11. Making Disciples — 39
12. How To Keep Your Invitation To Other Engaging — 43

13	Three Things Your Group Members Need (Including You)	47
14	Building Trust Within Your Small Group	49
15	Celebrate The Wins	51
16	Making Group Prayer A Priority	53
17	Balancing Social Time With Study Time	55
18	Providing Care Through Follow-Up	59
19	When Small Groups Feel Boring: Ten Ways To Change It Up	61
20	Three Questions To Answer Before Presenting To Groups	63
21	How To Ask Questions That Lead To Great Conversations	65
22	Did He Really Just Say?	69
23	Guiding An Awkward Conversation	73
24	When You Forget That God Never Forgets	77
25	Praying With Faith	81

1

SERVING IS LEADING

> "Some leaders may serve the Word, and leaders may serve tables, but all leaders serve"
>
> Acts 6[1]

Serving, by its very nature, is doing something that someone else is not doing. Any time you do something that no one else is doing you are providing a path to follow. Serving, by default, makes you an example. As you serve, you provide a model of leadership for others to follow.

Don't let anyone look down on you because you are young, but set an example for the believers in speech, in conduct, in love, in faith and in purity. **1 Timothy 4:12**

Young or old, live in such a way that your life is a model for others to follow as you follow Jesus. This was the Apostle Paul's desire:

Follow my example, as I follow the example of Christ. **1 Corinthians 11:1**

---

[1] *The Making of A Christian Leader*, pg. 41

SERVING IS SPIRIT LED

As each one has received a gift, minister it to one another, as good stewards (you've been entrusted with something that you originally did not possess) of the manifold grace of God. If anyone speaks, let him speak as the oracles of God (you are speaking on someone else's behalf). If anyone ministers, let him do it as with the ability which God supplies (you have power that you did not earn), that in all things God may be glorified through Jesus Christ (you are living for the exultation of a name that's not your own), to whom belong the glory and the dominion forever and ever. Amen. **1 Peter 4:10-11**

As a Christian leader your job is not to rely upon your own strengths and abilities but upon all that the Spirit of God makes available to you. Doing so will ensure that His work is completed and that His name is glorified.

SERVING IS WORSHIP

And whatever you do, do it heartily, as to the Lord and not to men, **Colossians 3:23**

Don't forget, you are serving God above man.

The Bible teaches that God lives within those who have placed their faith in Him but for a moment ask yourself, **"What if God was going to be there while I lead my small group?"**

Would you...

> Pray before it started?

> Prepare?

> Start on time?

> Look presentable?

We know that God is with us! But let's not forget that how we serve others is really how we serve Him.

Your commitment to use your gifts is ultimately made to God. Serve like you are truly serving Him.

I have a challenge for you:

Create and live in a **"get to"** environment, not a **"have to"** environment.

It is exhausting to live in a **"have to"** environment...

I have to work in a ministry.

Why does the church have to have multiple services?

I have to lead my small group.

Instead of living in a "have to" environment, what if you were committed to live in a "Why wouldn't I want to?" environment, realizing it is a privilege and honor to use the gifts God has placed within your life and to be a part of advancing His Kingdom in this earth.

2

RELIABILITY OVER QUALIFICATIONS

> It's one thing to be able to teach, it's another to be reliable.
>
> Unknown

Faithfulness is the great qualifier in God's kingdom. God uses those who are/will be faithful.

You then, my son, be strong in the grace that is in Christ Jesus. And the things you have heard me say in the presence of many witnesses entrust to reliable people who will also be qualified to teach others. Join with me in suffering, like a good soldier of Christ Jesus. No one serving as a soldier gets entangled in civilian affairs, but rather tries to please his commanding officer. Similarly, anyone who competes as an athlete does not receive the victor's crown except by competing according to the rules. The hardworking farmer should be the first to receive a share of the crops. Reflect on what I am saying, for the Lord will give you insight into all this.
2 Timothy 2:1-7

Paul gave Timothy some interesting instruction that may easily be missed at first glance in verse two. **There are two words that we should notice: *reliable* and *qualified*.** Before Timothy allows someone to teach he should first take a look at the character and uprightness of the individual.

How often do we assume the gift is enough to carry a person into leadership? How often do we see that the gift alone cannot keep an individual from falling from their place of leadership? It is a person's character and willingness to serve that will keep them in it for the long haul.

FAITHFULNESS is more important than QUALIFICATIONS.

Are you reliable?

Can you be you be trusted?

In the same passage the soldier, the athlete, and the farmer will only reap the rewards after the work has been put in.

To be considered faithful requires a track record of displaying loyalty and steadfastness towards a person, exercise, etc. When it comes to discipling others, faithfulness is a necessity. Think about this, Jesus chose twelve disciples in a day and then spent the next three years with them.

Evangelism comes quick. Discipleship can be slow.

Paul knew the right approach and understood his role in the task of discipleship: to be faithful. This principle is crystal clear in the following text:

What, after all, is Apollos? And what is Paul? Only servants, through whom you came to believe–as the Lord has assigned to each his task. I planted the seed, Apollos watered it, but God has been making it grow. So neither the one who plants nor the one who waters is anything, but only God, who makes things grow. The one who plants and the one who waters have one purpose, and they will each be rewarded according to their own labor. For we are co-workers in God's service; you are God's field, God's building. **1 Corinthians 3:5-9**

Discipleship is not an event, it is a life-long process. Whether a person allows you to walk with them for a day, a year or the next five decades, your job description will not change. Remain faithful.

3

PRIORITY AND PRACTICE OF BIBLE STUDY

Anyone who is sincere about growing spiritually must be willing to consistently spend time in God's Word by reading it and hearing teaching from it. The discipline of reading the Bible can be difficult to initiate if we do not understand why the Book was given to us, however, its purpose is discovered within its own text:

Then Jesus told him, "Because you have seen me, you have believed; blessed are those who have not seen and yet have believed." Jesus did many other miraculous signs in the presence of his disciples, which are not recorded in thisbook. But these are written that you may believe that Jesus is the Christ, the Son of God, and that by believing you may have life in his name. **John 20:29-31**

Belief in Jesus is vital to life, here on earth and eternally. The Bible teaches that Jesus is/gives life. A person can determine if they are experiencing "life" like the Bible describes by considering what their life resembles.

When examining areas of your life and even your small group ask yourself if those areas relate more closely to life or death? Are there areas that need to be nurtured and revitalized by the Word of God?

PRIORITY: Reading the Bible

The Word of God works within a person in the following ways to initiate His promise to us so that we can experience true life:

The Word of God...

✓ Feeds Our Spirit

✓ Transforms Our Mind

✓ Activates Us Into Action

Understanding that God's Word is life to the reader provides good reason for it to be read. The Bible is inspired by God. In Greek the word used is **theopneustos**[2], which literally translates: **God-breathed**.

There are basic elements of life that we cannot physically do without: air, food, and water. These things sustain the human body and allow a person to function correctly. Scripture compares these elements to the personhood of God.

Spiritually speaking, Scripture is breath, bread, and water to our spirit. The Bible also tells us that Jesus gives water and that He is bread. We also read that Jesus is the Word. Jesus is the perfect embodiment of the Bible and the Bible is the perfect embodiment of Jesus. When we read the Bible we are not just learning something but experiencing Someone, God.

If God's Word is breath, bread, and water for us, and if Jesus is the Word, how can we expect to know Him, become like Him, or lead others toward Him, if we do not read the Bible?

If you consider how long the human body can physically last without food, water, or air it is easy to connect how vital reading the Word of God

---

[2]"Greek Lexicon :: G2315 (KJV)." Blue Letter Bible. Sowing Circle. Web. 11 Mar, 2014. <http://www.blueletterbible.org/lang/lexicon/lexicon.cfm?Strongs=G2315&t=KJV>

should be to all people. Simply put, you will be unsatisfied if you do not read God's Word. Spiritually, without the Word, you will die.

PRACTICE: Learning the Bible

If one is going to truly learn a skill or understand an idea it will require practice. In the book of Romans the writer instructs the reader to offer their body as a sacrifice unto God.[3] A life that is submitted to God can be transformed and discern Gods will.

This process is referred to as sanctification. God is the one who completely cleanses and sets a person apart; however, obedience to God's Word through the power of the Holy Spirit allows this work to take place.

How can a person experience this work without daily application and practice of what they read? This is a purifying work that God performs for the good of those who believe. Though, potentially painful at times, it is an act of love so that the fruit of the believer's life will be more productive and beneficial to others. Consider this explanation of spiritual change:

"Sanctification is seen to be a continuing process throughout a Christian's entire lifetime. It is not something negative. A man is not considered holy because of the things he does not do. Virtue cannot be judged by the vices from which a person abstains. There must be a positive conformation to the image of Christ. This is seen as a gradual growth in, not into, grace..."[4]

This purifying process is one that every Christian should welcome and experience as they become obedient to the Word of God. The process begins with the gift of salvation. However, it is important to distinguish between receiving this gift and doing good works:

For by grace you have been saved through faith, and that not of yourselves; it is the gift of God, not of works, lest anyone should boast. For we are His workmanship, created in Christ Jesus for good works, which God prepared beforehand that we should walk in them. **Ephesians 2:8-10**

---

[3] Romans 12:1
[4] 4 Foundations of Pentecostal Theology, pg. 245

Salvation is a gift from God but upon receiving, intended for good works in the life of the Christian. Salvation is a saving work in three ways or tenses: Past, Present, and Future. Jesus Christ saves those who believe, from past sins and from the penalty that those sins warrant. Salvation from past sins is referred to as Justification. Faith in Jesus allows a person to stand righteous before God, the price has been paid, and the believer is justified before God because of Christ.

It is important as a leader and for those you lead to understand the difference between the past and present tense of salvation. "This is seen as a gradual growth in, not into, grace" meaning, a believer is already into grace, he is righteous. However, because a believer lives in the grace of God, they can grow in it or in other words, experience sanctification. Sanctification is the saving work of Christ that frees the believer from the power of sin and death on a daily basis.

In the book *Ethix*, Sean McDowell describes a conversation that he once had with a drunkard. The two were discussing the bible and the issue of freedom. During the talk the drunkard argued that he was free to drink; to do whatever he willed. To this Sean agreed but also asked the question, *"Are you free not to drink?"*

For the person who is growing and learning the ways of God, the beauty and power of His grace is displayed in the freedom to overcome, think differently, and to pursue what is honorable all because of, and through the gift of, salvation.

And lastly, trust in Christ will save the believer from the presence of sin when Jesus comes back a second time for His people. Glorification is described here:

Dear friends, now we are children of God, and what we will be has not yet been made known. But we know that when he appears, we shall be like him, for we shall see him as he is. **1 John 3:2**

How encouraging to know that Jesus is returning again on behalf of His people. The Bible teaches that God saves, enables, and transforms those who put their faith in Him. Applying the Word of God to your life will reveal His faithfulness and the truth of what is written in the Bible. Because of this, priority and focus should be placed upon reading and learning it.

4

USING YOUR TIME WISELY

Managing your time can be a challenging task. Life can become very busy between family, church culture, schooling, graduations, holidays, and oh yeah – work. Is it even possible to manage your time in a way where you are in control instead of the events and circumstances of life?

Sometimes it may feel like group time is just one more thing on the list of things to mark off. But, if you stop to think about why you lead groups and the benefits of it, you can overcome those feelings. Also, it may be that other things are cropping up in your life that are trying to choke out the fruitful work that you do for Gods kingdom.

The Bible instructs us to be wise in how we plan our day and live our life.

Be very careful, then, how you live–not as unwise but as wise, making the most of every opportunity, because the days are evil. Therefore do not be foolish, but understand what the Lord's will is. **Ephesians 5:15-17**

Here are a few suggestions that will serve you well if you're willing to be intentional when it comes to managing your time.

1. Establish Priorities

There is a basic guideline we can use when it comes to establishing priority: God first, Family second, and Ministry third.

There will always be things that are important but there will also always be things that are more important. When it comes to establishing priorities, determine what is most important in accordance to your relationship with God, your family, and ministry.

2. Use A Time Management Worksheet or Calendar

Writing down (or typing) how you plan to use your time for the day or week is an effective way to accomplish the things that are the most important to you. If you'd like to print a free time management worksheet, you can find one here: http://www.dailychristianhelp.com/wp-content/uploads/2014/12/time-management-worksheet.pdf.

How To Use The Time Management Worksheet

PART A: Identify Obligated Time

1. Fill in all of your responsibilities.

2. Fill in the hours you work

3. Fill in the time it takes to get ready and travel between home, school, and work.

4. Fill in any other regular appointments (church, transporting children, small group, etc.)

5. Fill in a breakfast, lunch and dinner break. Include time for food preparation.

6. Establish a set time to go to sleep and get up in the morning

PART B: Identify Free Time

1. Assign time for accomplishing the things that are the most important.

2. Allow adequate time for each priority that you establish as most important.

3. Schedule regular time with God and family.

PART C: Analyze Your Situation

1. Have you found "hidden time" you didn't know you had?

2. Is there enough time available to accomplish what is most important?

3. If your schedule cannot accommodate all the demands on your time, figure out what is not most important and remove from your schedule.

4. If your schedule looks reasonable, then stick to it!

With almost everyone having a smart phone, there is no reason not to use the calendar features available on your phone. There are also alerts and reminders that you can set so that you do not forget what you have scheduled.

Or, use an online calendars that allow you to share your calendar with your loved ones. If you're not technological, that's ok! Paper and pen work fine too. Use a wall calendar.

3. Delegate

Are there areas or responsibilities in your life that other people could help carry. Obviously, there are some areas that you cannot delegate, but some you can. The following questions are taken from the book, *The Making of a Christian Leader*, and will help you to determine what and if you should delegate.

1. Do you have little time for appointments, recreation, study, civil work, etc.?

2. Do you have unfinished jobs accumulating, or difficulty meeting deadlines?

3. Do you spend more of your time working on details than on planning and supervising?

4. Are you inclined to keep a finger in everything that is going on?

5. Do you hesitate to admit that you need help to keep on top of your job?

The following is a basic example for discovering a need you could delegate within your group:

Maybe at your group you like to always have food or something baked. Instead of you preparing food, cleaning the house, and facilitating, is there someone else in the group who could take care of bringing the food?

What ways or ideas could you begin to implement that will help you effectively use your time wisely for God's Kingdom?

5

What Exercise Reminded Me About Spiritual Growth?

> No matter how slow you go, you're still beating the guy sitting on the couch.
>
> Unknown

I recently noticed the above phrase posted on the bulletin board at the gym. There is so much encouragement and truth wrapped up in that little sentence. As I thought about the meaning, it hit me how comparable physical fitness and spiritual growth are.

Three things came to my mind as I compared the two disciplines:

1. There will always be an EXCUSE.

If you are anything like me than you can relate to the amount of times I have made excuses or have come up with other things to do (and I mean ANYTHING) rather than exercise. We have a way of making things that are not important seem as if they really are if it will help us get out of what we do not feel like doing. Or, in other words, are too LAZY to do.

This is true concerning spiritual disciplines as well. How often do we choose other things rather than spending time in prayer or reading the Bible? It's funny (or maybe not), that when I began writing this it was in the middle of my mandatory reading for school. Did I perhaps choose to write to get out of reading... maybe??

2. Accountability is NECESSARY.

There are certain days of the week that I know I will run into friends at the gym, they're always there and it is encouraging to me. We thrive off of each other. We want to see each other reach our goals. We can share advice and learn from one another.

In our spiritual walk few things are as important as accountability and Christian friendship. It is difficult to go against the current when you are the only one, but if there is a team surrounding you the destination is much more attainable. Accountability keeps us on course and true to our word, and His. Nothing will catapult a person quicker and farther than when they allow their self to be surrounded with people who care about them and who are also like-minded.

3. The more consistent you are the STRONGER you become.

Significant strides can be hard to notice unless viewed weeks or even months at a time when it comes to changing ones physique. However, over time one will notice that they can run farther, run faster, or even handle more weight; they have become stronger. This comes only through consistency and dedication, but the results are well worth it.

These kinds of strides are possible spiritually as well. No one should want to be the same person they were ten years ago, or to be the same ten years from now. This type of change is referred to in the church as "sanctification" but all that means is we are progressively being made into the image of God in character and love. This can be a painful process of self-sacrifice and self-examination but the fruit of our life will be much sweeter.

Small groups provide an excellent way to facilitate growth in each of those areas.

What similarities do you see between the two disciplines?

How could your small group encourage growth in these areas?

6

ARE YOU RESPONSIBLE FOR THE SPIRITUAL GROWTH OF OTHERS?

Spiritual Growth is a dynamic process that is highly personal yet involves others at the same time. As a group leader, what do you do and how should you feel when those in your group do not seem to be advancing or changing?

What role do you play in others growing spiritually and to what extent are you responsible?

The Bible provides needed insight into spiritual growth, here are some of the applicable verses:

Let us hold unswervingly to the hope we profess, for he who promised is faithful. And let us consider how we may spur one another on toward love and good deeds, not giving up meeting together, as some are in the habit of doing, but encouraging one another–and all the more as you see the Day approaching. **Hebrews 10:23-25**

Do nothing out of selfish ambition or vain conceit. Rather, in humility value others above yourselves, not looking to your own interests but each of you to the interests of the others. **Philippians 2:3-4**

Brothers and sisters, if someone is caught in a sin, you who live by the Spirit should restore that person gently. But watch yourselves, or you also may be tempted. Carry each other's burdens, and in this way you will fulfill the law of Christ. **Galatians 6:1-2**

Then Jesus came to them and said, "All authority in heaven and on earth has been given to me. Therefore go and make disciples of all nations, baptizing them in the name of the Father and of the Son and of the Holy Spirit, and teaching them to obey everything I have commanded you... **Matthew 28:18-20**

A believer in Jesus Christ is expected to disciple others, but are they personally responsible for the growth that does or does not occur in those they are discipling?

A group leader (and all Christians) are responsible to help facilitate and encourage spiritual growth in others but growth will only occur in accordance with the persons desire to grow.

The Apostle Paul expresses this same issue in his letters to the Corinthian church. His intense awareness of their immaturity was a reason for the letters.

In the following passage we can gather a liberating truth about discipling others:

So neither the one who plants nor the one who waters is anything, but only God, who makes things grow. The one who plants and the one who waters have one purpose, and they will each be rewarded according to their own labor. For we are co-workers in God's service; you are God's field, God's building. **1 Corinthians 3:7-8**

A group leader's job is to plant and to water. Only God and the individual decide if their heart will be receptive ground for receiving what you offer.

Sometimes, as a leader we put expectations on those around us or have results in mind that we think should be reached by a certain point. Without expressing these expectations, frustration is inevitable. The fact is, people do not always want to change or may be unsure of how to change.

When our motivation for discipling others becomes about seeing results that we desire rather than simply pointing them toward Jesus and to His character we will end up confused or exhausted.

A *results* based approach to discipleship will cause you to teach people what you want them to know instead of what God has already done for them.

People know what it looks like to live better. Most people are already aware of what they need to stop and need to start.

People need to be settled in their belief about Christ. When people believe Christ and are pointed toward what He has already done, it will do more to advance spiritual growth than teaching them what they need to do differently.

This does not hinder us from defining what a win would look like in a certain area or from providing practical steps for that person to take to achieve victory. It is often necessary to clarify how to live as a Christian for those you are discipling.

As a group leader you are called to cultivate, encourage, and prepare opportunity for spiritual growth to take place. What others do with the water you pour out or the seed you plant is up to them.

I pray that you would remain encouraged in Christ and that the passion God has placed within you would continue to burn even in the times when discipleship seems slow.

Are there more responsibilities that you can think of besides the core essentials that I shared?

7

HOW TO HELP OTHERS GROW SPIRITUALLY

In the last chapter it was pointed out that discipleship is a multi-faceted process that involves God, leaders, and individuals. A leader who desires to disciple others is responsible *"to cultivate, encourage, and prepare opportunity for spiritual growth to take place."*

But what about those who attend your group? What steps should they personally take to receive the most benefit from a small group setting and from those who care about their spiritual growth?

As a group leader you can encourage group members to consistently put the following practices into place to help foster their own spiritual growth:

1. Own It!

Therefore, my brothers and sisters, make every effort to confirm your calling and election. For if you do these things, you will never stumble, and you will receive a rich welcome into the eternal kingdom of our Lord and Savior Jesus Christ. **2 Peter 1:10-11**

Without reading the other verses surrounding those, it would seem as if a believer must strive and work all on their own to grow in their faith. But verse three reveals where a Christian's strength truly comes from when they are willing to rely on Christ:

His divine power has given us everything we need for a godly life through our knowledge of him who called us by his own glory and goodness. **2 Peter 1:3**

Because of the power that is available to us we should point those in our group toward Christ, in and for all situations. Again, people need to be settled in their belief about Christ. When people believe Christ and are pointed toward what Christ has already done, it will do more to advance spiritual growth within them than teaching them what they need to do differently.

When we are sure of who Christ is and what He has done, it will lead us to more willingly turn toward Him for everything.

2. Participate!

For just as each of us has one body with many members, and these members do not all have the same function, so in Christ we, though many, form one body, and each member belongs to all the others. **Romans 12:4-5**

Every person in the Body of Christ is responsible to one-another (and ultimately, God) to share what God has entrusted to them. Small groups are a way to help facilitate connection and to share what God is doing in our life.

Encouraging participation is key to helping others to grow. Joining in group discussion, helping prepare for the night, bringing snacks, greeting at the door, leading prayers, outreach, or sharing an evening out as a group are all ways to be a participant.

Invite those who attend your group to share in the responsibilities and opportunities to participate.

3. Be Honest!

Therefore each of you must put off falsehood and speak truthfully to your neighbor, for we are all members of one body. **Ephesians 4:25 25**

As the leader you can encourage honesty by leading the way by being transparent and accountable too. As you model this for those in your group, it will encourage them to do the same which will lead to deeper conversation, prayer, and accountability.

8

HOW A GROUP ENVIRONMENT CAN FACILITATE SPIRITUAL GROWTH

In the last couple of chapters we looked at the personal responsibility each person should assume concerning growing spiritually and how as the leader you can model what that looks like for those in your group.

Now let's look at three ways a healthy group can foster and support Christian community and growth.

Again, remember the purpose of small groups is to help the Body of Christ at large and local churches to experience community and grow spiritually. This is essentially two sides to one coin. As individuals gather together in the context of Christian friendship and biblical principles, spiritual growth is inevitable.

When a person is intentional about being around and forming Christian friendship, it naturally paves the way for Christian spiritual growth to occur.

As a group leader, you can have confidence that growth will take place by ensuring that the following three elements are continuously incorporated into your group:

1. TRUST

Group members should be able to trust each other in the following ways:

- That there is genuine care for each other.
- That what is shared will not be used to slander or gossip about them.
- That misunderstanding or miscommunication can be worked out.

2. ENCOURAGEMENT

Group members should encourage one another in the following ways:

- To live according to the Word of God.
- To change as God directs and moves them.
- To use the gifts God has placed within their lives.

3. LOVE

Group members should experience Christ-like love in the following ways:

Love is patient, love is kind. It does not envy, it does not boast, it is not proud. It does not dishonor others, it is not self-seeking, it is not easily angered, it keeps no record of wrongs. Love does not delight in evil but rejoices with the truth. It always protects, always trusts, always hopes, always perseveres. **1 Corinthians 13:4-7**

Is your group intentional about incorporating these elements into your time together?

How could your group experience trust, encouragement, and love in a greater way?

9

WHY MULTIPLICATION MATTERS

Whether your group recently started meeting or has been together for a while, it is important to build your group with multiplication in mind. Your group may feel that the chemistry is "just right" which can makes the thought of change difficult. However, multiplying your group will promote health and cause growth not just for others but for you as well.

As you grow together as a group, grow with the understanding that **Multiplication Matters**. Below are a few reasons why you should pray for, build upon, and lead toward multiplication:

1. Jesus Commanded That We Multiply

Jesus commissioned His disciples to go and make other disciples.

Then Jesus came to them and said, "All authority in heaven and on earth has been given to me. Therefore go and make disciples of all nations, baptizing them in the name of the Father and of the Son and of the Holy Spirit, and teaching them to obey everything I have commanded you. And surely I am with you always, to the very end of the age. **Matthew 28:18-20**

How easy would it have been for the disciples to just remain in their group? They had grown to know each other, they knew each other's weaknesses, and had experienced things together that were unique to their relationship. Regardless, they were more committed to fulfilling the instruction of their Master.

Jesus modeled a pattern of discipleship:

- The one whom Jesus loved, John (John 13:23 and 20:2)

- Peter, James, and John were invited to the Transfiguration (Luke 9:28)

- The twelve disciples were sent out (Matthew 10)

- The seventy two were sent out (Luke 10)

2. Multiplication Gives The Group A Goal

Having a goal to multiply will be a good reminder of one of the reasons for the group. This goal will provide a source of unity for your group. Having a goal in a group environment will naturally cause the members to work together providing opportunity for growth in and through those who participate in achieving the goal.

It is also reasonable to keep in mind that groups have a life span. Allow your group to live and breathe but be aware when it is time to mix things up by multiplying (this is one reason why identifying leaders within your small group is important). This is one way to ensure that your group will end strong.

3. Multiplication Provides Opportunity For Others To Experience Community And Grow Spiritually

Multiplying your group provides new opportunities for outsiders to share in authentic Christian relationship. Adding new members to a group will also inject new energy, perspective, conversation, and diversity–all of which will be fresh air to a group that is nearing the time for multiplication.

As a group leader, I encourage you to pray for and take action concerning multiplication within your small group. Let's pray together that we would see additional groups form. Let's commit together to multiply our groups by investing in leaders and inviting those who are on the outside to join in by sharing life, God, and prayer together.

10

IDENTIFYING LEADERSHIP WITHIN YOUR SMALL GROUP

One of the keys to multiplication is to remember the opportunity that you have to replace yourself by preparing others for leadership.

Here are a few ways that you can begin to make this special investment into someone else, so that multiplication, rather than just addition, takes place within your small group.

1. Pray. Ask God to help you with the process.

Identify those who model Godly character and share faith in Jesus Christ.

Once these two foundational qualities have been identified further consider:

- Do their strengths display the capability to lead others in a group environment?

- Is the person an active participant in church?

- Do they share the mission of the local church?

- Are they open to teaching and training?

2. Begin to share responsibility with them.

- Ask them to greet at the door as group members arrive.

- Let them open the group with prayer.

- Ask them to do follow-up during the week.

- Walk them through the process of how you prepare for a small group meeting.

One of the primary responsibilities of small group leaders should be to mentor, train and release other small group leaders.

Jesus modeled this example by releasing others to use their God-given talents and abilities.

Keep in mind, you are not trying to find someone who can lead a group tonight, but someone you can train and teach to lead well in the future.

How are you being intentional by investing in other potential leaders within your group?

11

Making Disciples

Discipleship is where the rubber meets the road when it comes to multiplication. It is one thing to identify leaders and have a heart to multiply, but discipleship is the process that allows both of those goals to be reached.

Another reason for small groups is to help facilitate the process of discipling believers. You should want to help people experience community and grow spiritually as a result of participating in your small group.

You may agree with me that small groups are a great model to use to accomplish that task, but this work will only be accomplished by people who engage in the mission to disciple others.

Concerning discipleship Leroy Eims wrote:

The ministry is to be carried on by people, not programs. It is to be carried out by someone and not by something.[5]

For you or maybe your church, small groups is the "thing" that you are using but the desired results can only be accomplished through people who are committed to the goal to lead others closer to Jesus.

The following are a few more principles taken from the book, *The Lost Art of Disciple Making*, by Leroy Eims.

---

[5] The Lost Art Of Disciple Making, pg. 45

"In selecting men and women (to disciple), you'll have to abandon proneness to conformity and follow the example of Jesus."[6]

Jesus did not ask men to follow Him who were exactly like Him. He chose men with different interests, different backgrounds, and different personalities. Discipling those who are not exactly like you will cause you to grow along with those you are discipling.

"When you are training potential disciples and workers, let them in on some of the trials and tribulations of the ministry that you have faced."[7]

There is a reason why Jesus invited some of the disciples to come a little closer the night He was betrayed in the garden of Gethsemane. He knew that if they were going to truly carry on the work of the ministry, they would need to know that difficulty is real and Who could see them through.

"To get people involved in a discipleship ministry and to help them become disciples, three things are necessary initially. They must be motivated to become disciples, they must have regular fellowship with Jesus Christ, and they must witness to Him."[8]

These traits are necessary because you can't disciple someone who doesn't want to be. They must understand that Jesus is ultimately their teacher, not you.

And lastly, a disciple must know that sharing their faith is fruit that bears from a relationship with God. He is the One who enables and provides the power to do so.

Jesus taught us that we must remain in Him to be productive disciples:

Remain in me, as I also remain in you. No branch can bear fruit by itself; it must remain in the vine. Neither can you bear fruit unless you remain in me. I am the vine; you are the branches. If you remain in me and I in you, you will bear much fruit; apart from me you can do nothing.

---

[6] The Lost Art Of Disciple Making, pg. 30
[7] The Lost Art Of Disciple Making, pg. 35
[8] The Lost Art Of Disciple Making, pg. 51

John 15:4-5

Again back to Eims's book:

"For your life to transmit effectively, two things are required: availability and transparency."[9]

A natural occurrence will take place within a group setting as life stories and prayer requests are shared; community will deepen. A key element in any healthy community is a willingness to be there for those involved, not just during group time but even outside of the meeting. Honesty is also crucial in order to move beyond the surface to deeper areas of trust and accountability.

As a leader, in order to transfer what is important to you (and to Jesus) into the lives of others, you must model what you hope to see in them.

Discipleship requires the leader to be available and transparent.

"You must help the potential worker develop a heart for people. It is so easy to fall into the trap of looking on people as a means to an end, a means of accomplishing an objective or fulfilling a vision."[10]

No one had/has a bigger heart for people or a bigger vision to reach people than Jesus. Jesus never lost touch of His love for people and was always careful to instill this same passion in His followers. This is evident in the following verses:

Jerusalem, Jerusalem, you who kill the prophets and stone those sent to you, how often I have longed to gather your children together, as a hen gathers her chicks under her wings, and you were not willing. **Matthew 23:37**

A new command I give you: Love one another. As I have loved you, so you must love one another. ³⁵*By this everyone will know that you are my disciples, if you love one another.* **John 13:34-35**

---

[9]The Lost Art Of Disciple Making, pg. 100
[10]The Lost Art Of Disciple Making, pg. 110

The Apostle Paul modeled this same manner of love for those he invested into:

We were not looking for praise from people, not from you or anyone else, even though as apostles of Christ we could have asserted our authority. Instead, we were like young children among you. Just as a nursing mother cares for her children, so we cared for you. Because we loved you so much, we were delighted to share with you not only the gospel of God but our lives as well. **1 Thessalonians 2:6-8**

Every word and action should be motivated and driven by the love of God in the life of a believer. People should never become a means to an end. God does not ask us to make robots, but disciples. Disciples are people, people that God loves more than you or I ever could.

Does discipleship provide the framework for your life and small group?

What are some ideas that you could incorporate into your life to more effectively disciple others?

12

How To Keep Your Invitation To Other Engaging

One question that I'm sometimes asked is, "How do I get people to come to my small group?"

As a small group leader you should be intentional about inviting others to be a part of your group. Often time's group leaders think that people will just magically show up for a meeting or that the church should get the people there. You should assume total responsibility for the success of your group.

Below are a few ways successful group leaders have used to invite people and to keep their group as a topic of conversation amongst their friends, coworkers, neighbors, and family members.

1. Personally Invite People

Among all the other suggestions that will be provided this is the most important one to remain consistent. Nothing communicates interest in another person like face to face interaction. I recently came across this post from Erwin McManus on Instagram about how drawing closer to people is directly related to growing closer to God.

If you are like me (comfortable in solitude), then you may need to be more intentional about going out of your way to invite people to come to your group. Even if they never come, they will know that you care, which could lead to later opportunity.

You could make cards about your group to give to people. Invite your co-workers. Encourage your friends to spend an hour of their week with you. God may lay a person on your heart or prompt you to invite someone who currently does not know about or attend your group. Sometimes this may mean stepping out of your "comfort zone" but this is how we grow and the benefits for both you and the one invited could be great!

2. Use Social Media

Social media, like many other mediums, can be used for good or bad. If you already use Facebook, Twitter, Instagram, or blog, why not use it as a platform to let others know what God is doing in your life? Remember though, the people we lead determine the credibility of our message by the content of our lives.

While social media can be a great way to connect and provide resources, it also serves as a window into your life beyond your ministry involvement. In light of that, you should always use social media purposefully with others in mind so that God's character is displayed.

I have a friend that has used twitter to share updates about their group night. It is always encouraging to read his tweets about their time together.

Do you have a Facebook account? Facebook can be a great way to share what is going on in your group and to create interest in others about what you're doing. Some group leaders use Facebook to celebrate and share what God is doing in their group.

Those are just a couple of great examples of how you could use social media to promote your group and let others know that they too could experience community and grow spiritually.

3. Use Email

Another friend of mine uses his email list to let those in his circle know when he is hosting a group. Email also makes it super easy for others to forward your small group information on to the people they think would be interested.

This friend would send an initial email containing information about an upcoming group he and his wife were hosting. And then on a once a week basis he would send out a review of the groups discussion followed by a brief preview about the topic for next week.

4. Pray For God To Send The Right People To Your Group

One of the ushers at my church also leads a men's group and has specifically prayed for God to send the right men to his group, and God has sent guys who needed to be there.

5. Send A Note

Write a letter, send a postcard, etc. to let those connected to you know that you are leading a group and would like for them to be a part.

Whether you realize it or not God has given you a sphere of influence (your family, workplace, neighborhood, apartment complex, church).

Allow where God has placed you to be an opportunity to invite others into what God is doing!

There is a familiar phrase that says, *People don't care what you know until they know that you care.* Inviting others to be a part of your group is a great way to let them know that you care.

What about you? How do you keep your invitation to others new and engaging? I'd love to hear how you keep your invitation at the forefront. You can send your responses to me at:

Twitter: @EvanDoyletweets   Facebook: theEvanDoyle
Email: evan@dailychristianhelp.com

13

THREE THINGS YOUR GROUP MEMBERS NEED (INCLUDING YOU)

Do you ever find yourself unsure of how to meet the needs of those in your group? The issues, difficulties, prayer requests, and problems that we all face can feel overwhelming when you're not sure of what to say or do.

This chapter will narrow down three main things that all group members need no matter what circumstances are being faced.

Every Person Needs:

1. Affection

This is love: not that we loved God, but that he loved us and sent his Son as an atoning sacrifice for our sins. Dear friends, since God so loved us, we also ought to love one another. **1 John 4:10-11**

In the same manner that God loves us, we should love each other. It is so important to know that you are loved.

Godly love is displayed when our words and actions draw others closer to God. This means that what we say and do toward others are a reflection of God's heart and character.

2. Protection

Brothers and sisters, if someone is caught in a sin, you who live by the Spirit should restore that person gently. But watch yourselves, or you also may be tempted. Carry each other's burdens, and in this way you will fulfill the law of Christ. **Galatians 6:1-2**

As a group (and as the Body of Christ in general) we should help each other through our troubles.

3. Connection

For just as each of us has one body with many members, and these members do not all have the same function, so in Christ we, though many, form one body, and each member belongs to all the others. **Romans 12:4-5**

Every person has something to offer to the Body of Christ. Actually, we are responsible to share and contribute what God has entrusted to us. The Body of Christ is connected through the work of Jesus Christ. Remember that disagreement, color, economic status, background, etc. should never be barrier between brothers and sisters in Christ.

Who do you know that needs to receive one of these elements of Christian fellowship? How could you meet that need?

14

BUILDING TRUST WITHIN YOUR SMALL GROUP

If your group has been meeting consistently for at least a month or two then you have probably engaged in conversation on a deeper level than just talking about lasts weeks sporting events or where you work.

When conversation moves to places beyond just the average chit/chat, more than just details are surfacing, trust is being displayed.

The word trust means belief that someone or something is reliable, good, honest, effective, etc.

When someone shares with you or in a group setting, they are doing more than just getting something off of their chest, they are revealing that they put stock in who you are as a person. Don't miss what I just said.

Here are a few ways to build trust and promote honesty within your group:

***Avoid judgment and criticism.** Plain and simple.

***Show appreciation when someone opens up.** You could say something like, "Thank you for sharing that."

***Allow people to share at their own pace.** Attempting to force someone to talk, read, or pray will often times push them farther away from connectivity.

*Share the truth in love. Being a great leader demands the willingness to share truth. Openness should never come at the expense of the truth. When an honest answer is needed respond with the love of Christ – measuring every word.

*Realize when what is being shared does not add value to the whole group. Occasionally, you will need to refocus the conversation to the topic at hand. The other members of your group will appreciate this ten times over and place trust in you as a leader. They will also be more open to share instead of counting down the minutes until they can leave.

There may be times when a person shares issues they are facing that are of a very serious nature, such as: end of life situations, a serious medical diagnosis or pending surgery, suicidal thoughts, marriage problems, addiction issues, a family crisis, etc. It is a good idea to have a list of resources that you can turn to that can provide further help for special situations. Your church may already have a list of contacts that you could use. If not, maybe you could be the one to help assemble one.

What are some ways that you could use to build trust and honesty within your group?

15

CELEBRATE THE WINS

WINNING IS FUN!

Recently I witnessed this first hand as my oldest son's baseball team was crowned champions of a weekend tournament. It was awesome for them to experience the reward of practicing and not giving up even when the game became difficult. At some points it even appeared as if his team might lose. It was an emotional game for them and even for the spectators (especially the parents).

Winning is the desired culmination of all the effort that is put toward achieving a goal. For a small group leader, the win will look a little different than what it will for a baseball team but nevertheless the victory is just as sweet.

An important aspect of spiritual growth is celebrating the victories. Doing so reminds us to focus on the reason for the group by placing value on the life change God brings about in people. It's important to take time to celebrate these within your group.

A victory in a small group setting may be any of the following among lots of others:

- Someone sharing for the first time

- Answered prayer requests

- Deeper friendship within the group

- Approaching a circumstance with scriptural perspective

- A godly change in attitude or priorities

Take a minute to pinpoint some victories that have taken place within your group. What are they and how could you celebrate them within your group?

16

Making Group Prayer A Priority

It may seem obvious why praying together in your small group matters, but below are a few central reasons for making sure that prayer is always a part of your time together. Your group should provide opportunity to share life, God, and prayer together!

1. Sharing prayer requests strengthens community.

It is amazing the impact sharing a prayer request can have on drawing a group together. The essence of a prayer reveals matters that are beyond surface conversation.

When someone shares matters that they are praying about they are sharing things about their life that they care the most about.

As a small group, one of the goals is to experience community. True community is able to take place among open and honest people.

As a group, care for and gather around the prayers that are shared.

2. Prayer is an intentional invitation for God to lead your group.

When we pray we are asking God to intervene, lead, and guide our lives. Wouldn't we want the same for our small group? When we pray we are recognizing that God knows better, has more power, and is able to do what we have not been able.

Do not be anxious about anything, but in every situation, by prayer and petition, with thanksgiving, present your requests to God. And the peace of God, which transcends all understanding, will guard your hearts and your minds in Christ Jesus. **Philippians 4:6-7**

Prayer reminds us that God is in control and that we don't have to be.

3. Prayer allows God to work.

Answered prayer, even when it may not be the way we hoped, encourages faith and inspires you to trust God in all circumstances. When a group prays together, everyone has opportunity for their relationship with God to grow and be strengthened.

Now to Him who is able to do immeasurably more than all we ask or imagine, according to His power that is at work within us... **Ephesians 3:20**

Think about the amazing power that God says He will use on behalf of those who believe and pray according to His Will!

In order to incorporate prayer into your group, you must do so purposefully. In doing so you are truly making way for God to do great things in and through your group. Praying together is an important aspect of experiencing community and growing spiritually. If you are not already, decide now to intentionally make it a part of your group life.

How has prayer impacted your group?

17

BALANCING SOCIAL TIME WITH STUDY TIME

Groups will always offer a great opportunity to spend time and have fun with each other. But have you ever finished a group night and thought, *"What a great time, but what about the bible study?"* If so, this more than likely means that you are experiencing community within your group.

But what about growing spiritually? There will always be a challenge to balance between experiencing community and growing spiritually within your group.

Relationship can be so refreshing when it is with healthy and mature adults who are heading in the same direction as you are. God not only wants us to be connected with others but also with HIM. Our relationship with each other should be intentional.

Our friendship with each other should also deepen our relationship with the Lord. This comes through intentionally discussing, sharing, and studying Gods Word and our relationship with Him.

Group leaders should strive to have a healthy balance within their group of experiencing community and growing spiritually.

Here are four tips that you can put into practice:

1. Make the most of time outside of group to deepen relationships.

As you spend time with people during group, it will naturally develop into friendship outside of group as well. Using the extra time that you have throughout the month or week is a great way to get together with those within your group outside of group time. This will help free up more time to intentionally pray and study God's Word together during group.

2. Express clear expectations for your group time.

Make it clear from the beginning that your group time will primarily consist of two things: experiencing community (connecting relationally) and growing spiritually (connecting with God through prayer and study of His Word). Don't hesitate to pull your group back in by reminding them of this goal.

3. Describe what spiritual growth looks like.

Help your group members to understand how connecting relationally goes hand in hand with growing spiritually (2 Timothy 3:16-17, Hebrews 10:23-25, Proverbs 27:17). Consider setting aside some time during group to discuss how each person is growing spiritually and also how your group as whole is growing.

4. Move beyond "what"?

It is natural for people to come to group with the hope of getting things off of their chest. Openness within your group is a good thing but don't allow the conversations to remain at "what".

Help the "what's" to progress to questions like "so what?" and "now what?"

Always affirm how your group members feel, but also ask questions in a way that will help provide solutions.

"It must be difficult having a co-worker who talks to you that way. What do you think would be a Christ-like way to respond when people hurt you?"

Learning to ask "so what" and "now what" questions takes practice, but will always be worth it in the context of your group.

Have you found your group putting more emphasis on social time while neglecting study time? What actions could you take to change the pattern?

18

Providing Care Through Follow-Up

Providing care is another key to having a successful small group. This key focuses on how to provide care in small and big ways. One of the ways to provide care as a small group leader is by following up with those who attend your group. Doing so creates opportunity for deeper ministry and communicates that you care about those who attend your group.

Below are a few questions to ask yourself that may indicate the need to follow up with group members:

"Did someone leave group and still seem to be carrying something that was heavy upon them?"

"Did someone ask for prayer, or share about a meeting, an interview, a need, or something that was time sensitive to that week?"

If so, checking in with them to see how things went is a great way to further encourage and support them during that time.

"Is there something that took place that requires more information or needs to be acted upon?"

"How did the overall group seem? We're they engaged and responsive?"

By being aware of the answers to questions like those provided will further ensure your ability to provide care for your group. Follow-up is a simple way to communicate that you care, and to share the character and heart of God.

While there are many ways to follow up with people (email, text, Facebook, etc.) a personal contact where they hear your voice is always best.

What questions could you ask that would help you to determine if there is a need for follow up?

How could you effectively follow up with members of your group?

19

When Small Groups Feel Boring: Ten Ways To Change It Up

Go ahead, admit it. Sometimes small group can feel a little boring. Small groups provide a unique opportunity for people to gather, share, and grow together in a safe setting. Remember your goal is to experience community and grow spiritually within your group. However, there are times throughout the life of a small group that it can become monotonous or even feel boring.

When this happens it is time to mix it up a little bit. When a group begins to feel stale, it doesn't necessarily means that it is time to end, the group may just need to make a slight adjustment to help breathe new life throughout the group.

Below are ten easy ways to change it up when small group feels boring:

1. Plan a fun night or event.

2. Pray together.

3. Choose a new place to meet long term.

4. Meet at a different location one time.

5. Have a night that incorporates worship.

6. Eat a meal together.

7. Have a testimony night.

8. Study through the book of Proverbs.

9. Serve as a group at a church event or outreach.

10. Take a step back and recall why you lead a small group.

Do you have some other ideas for ways you change it up? If so, write them down below. Even if you don't use then right away they will be here waiting for when you need them.

20

THREE QUESTIONS TO ANSWER BEFORE PRESENTING TO GROUPS

If you've prepared for leading a group, teaching a sermon, or giving a presentation then you've probably asked yourself, **"What am I going to talk about?"**

Even if you use study guides or curriculums you are still responsible to share a clear message with applicable points for real life.

A great way to steer your thoughts and notes, as you prayerfully consider what you should share or what the conversation should accomplish, is by asking yourself these three guiding questions:

WHAT?
SO WHAT?
NOW WHAT?

1. WHAT?

WHAT DO I WANT PEOPLE TO KNOW?

Whether it is a sermon, a presentation, or guiding a small group discussion it is important to give clear direction for where you are headed. This will help people to engage quicker and to stay on topic with you.

Defining **"WHAT?"** to your group means that you are telling them about the main subject or theme.

You are simply beginning by stating what it is you will be talking about.

2. SO WHAT?

WHY DOES THIS MATTER TO THEIR LIFE?

With each point that you make or idea that you have to inspire thought and conversation, you should have the intention of conveying why it is important for those who are listening or engaged in the conversation. By answering **"SO WHAT?"** you are providing evidence that what you are talking about matters to those listening.

Preparing with the first two steering questions in mind, WHAT? and SO WHAT?, will help you to answer and present what it is you are talking about and why it is important for those listening. The third question is equally important.

3. NOW WHAT?

HOW CAN AND SHOULD THIS BE APPLIED?

A call to action provides people with the steps that they need to successfully apply the WHAT? and SO WHAT? of your discussion or message. Answering **"NOW WHAT?"** with clear steps or challenges will foster growth and maturity as people apply what they now know.

Having a call to action also provides accountability and causes one to be responsible with what they have learned.

21

HOW TO ASK QUESTIONS THAT LEAD TO GREAT CONVERSATIONS

Nothing will leave you wanting to learn how to ask great questions more than an awkward, short exchange of boring inquiries that result in simple answers.

We've all been there, wanting to take the conversation deeper to a more interesting level but unsure how to go about it.

Below are three quick tips that will breathe new life into your discussions as you learn to ask better questions that promote even better conversation.

1. Ask questions that demand more than one word answers.

Imagine the length and quality of a conversation based upon questions that allow yes or no answers.

- Do you love Jesus?

- Is it hard to be where you work?

- Are your kids doing well in school?
- Do you serve at church?
- Are you developing Christian friendship?

Now, think about the possibilities for a conversation if the questions were slightly tweaked.

- Why do you love Jesus?
- What about your job makes it difficult?
- How are your kids adjusting this year?
- What keeps you from using your talents at church?
- In what ways has having Christian friends impacted your life?

Do you notice the difference?

Even if you continue to receive short answers from open-ended questions you still have a lot more to work with than a question that allows for a one word answer.

2. Ask questions that lead to discussion about application.

Meaningful conversations contain the opportunity for growth and action. Chances are if a conversation contains questions then new perspective can be discovered and learning can possibly take place. These are moments that can lead to asking questions about how to take what has been discussed and put it into action. Which in turn leads to more follow up questions based upon how the application process went.

3. Ask questions based on what you've already heard. (This means you need to listen.)

Rather than rigidly sticking to an agenda, ask questions that are based on what has been shared which will allow for deeper conversation.

This is a sure-fire way to communicate that you care and are listening to what others are saying.

The next you time you have the opportunity to ask questions, do so out of a desire to know the other person better and to communicate that you care. Think of the questions that you ask as an intentional way to inspire growth and not just as a means to get an answer.

22

DID HE REALLY JUST SAY?

The health of your relationships will directly affect your influence as a leader. This will hold true and have power to impact positively or negatively depending on the condition of your relationships.

When my wife and I were first married, we regularly attended young married events that were similar to a small group environment. The events typically started off relaxed with everyone just hanging out. Later in the evening a teaching would be presented followed by group discussion.

I'll never forget the time when a couple was sharing that the husband called his wife a bonehead. The conversation came to a screeching halt and even worse the wife shut down. And who could blame her. I'm certain that if you could see what people were thinking it would have been, "Did he really just say that?!" Everyone there witnessed firsthand that *"Words kill, words give life; they're either poison or fruit–you choose."*[11]

A couple of the values and goals that should be shared within the group are **1) Trust:** In order for members of the group to be authentic, they must know that what they have discussed will not be shared as gossip. **2) Respect:** Members of the group will display honor by not saying anything that will embarrass or put down their spouse or other members.

---
[11] Proverbs 18:21 (MSG Bible)

Here are three easy ways to promote health within your relationships and will be a model to those you lead through the words that you share:

1. Always, always honor your spouse.

A wife desires to be esteemed. A husband should always hold his wife in high regard.

Husbands should esteem their wife in word and action, even in public. This communicates honor to her and others.

Husbands, in the same way be considerate as you live with your wives, and treat them with respect as the weaker partner and as heirs with you of the gracious gift of life, so that nothing will hinder your prayers. **1 Peter 3:7**

Husbands thrive on respect. Wives should ask, "Am I communicating respect through my words and actions?"

However, each one of you also must love his wife as he loves himself, and the wife must respect her husband. **Ephesians 5:33**

2. Agree beforehand what will be shared.

Again, this applies more specifically to married couples but is also applicable to other relationships.

Trust takes time to build but can be broken in an instant. Even though group environments are meant to inspire openness, there are times where some things are better kept reserved, at least for a time.

As a couple, one way to safeguard against sharing before the other is ready is by first expressing to one another how much you want said, if anything at all, and also asking if it is ok to share about details or circumstances.

3. Be aware of your motives.

At least two things should be considered when it comes to sharing information about another person:

Intent: *"Is what I'm sharing meant to make me look like the better person? Am I sharing this to tear another person down?"*

Content: Even though something may be true or really did take place, it is not always helpful to share with others about it. Will what you share embarrass or shame the one you talking about? Gossip should have no place in our conversations but only that which is helpful and edifying. The Bible in multiple places condemns practicing gossip.[12]

As a group leader, spouse, friend, co-worker, neighbor, member of the body of Christ, etc. our words should be used to draw one another closer to God as we apply scripture to our lives:

Do not let any unwholesome talk come out of your mouths, but only what is helpful for building others up according to their needs, that it may benefit those who listen. **Ephesians 4:29**

How have you seen the positive effects of speaking well of others impact a relationship or group?

---

[12]Romans 1:29-32, 1 Timothy 5:12-13, Proverbs 20:19

23

GUIDING AN AWKWARD CONVERSATION

It doesn't take long in a group setting for a challenging or uncomfortable conversation to take place. As a group leader, how should you guide the conversation to make sure that it remains fruitful and on task?

Rather than wondering what you should have said or what others must have been thinking, be proactive in leading the conversation by keeping the following tips in mind:

1. Pray

Additional prayer is always good but especially when a discussion begins to take place that enters into deep waters or controversial subjects. When this happens begin praying. Ask God for wisdom, truth, and discernment.

If any of you lacks wisdom, you should ask God, who gives generously to all without finding fault, and it will be given to you. But when you ask, you must believe and not doubt, because the one who doubts is like a wave of the sea, blown and tossed by the wind. **James 1:5-6**

Knowing when to continue a conversation or to stop it and what to say requires the wisdom of God.

2. Is it fruitful?

Another way to determine if a conversation is worth continuing is by asking yourself if it is fruitful? The following scriptures provide boundaries for the conversations that we engage in. Although the topic itself may be all together good, it is important to determine if talking about it is producing spiritual fruit.

Finally, brothers and sisters, whatever is true, whatever is noble, whatever is right, whatever is pure, whatever is lovely, whatever is admirable–if anything is excellent or praiseworthy–think about such things. **Philippians 4:8**

But the fruit of the Spirit is love, joy, peace, forbearance, kindness, goodness, faithfulness, gentleness and self-control. Against such things there is no law. **Galatians 5:22-23**

Even though the specific subject may not be inherently wrong we should be careful to notice the manner in which it is being discussed and if it is relevant to the group, and not just an individual.

3. Balance everything with the Word of God.

Ultimately, God's Word should always be the source that we use to uphold teaching and ways of thinking. The Bible is given to us so that we can know God and His heart in a deeper way and to equip us to live according to it.

And this is my prayer: that your love may abound more and more in knowledge and depth of insight, so that you may be able to discern what is best and may be pure and blameless for the day of Christ, filled with the fruit of righteousness that comes through Jesus Christ–to the glory and praise of God. **Philippians 1:9-11**

All Scripture is God-breathed and is useful for teaching, rebuking, correcting and training in righteousness, so that the servant of God may be thoroughly equipped for every good work. **2 Timothy 3:16-17**

Knowing what the Bible says is important for determining if what is being said is true, applicable, and worth discussing.

Is there an ongoing topic within your group that these principles could help steer the conversation to a healthy place? If so, begin applying these practices the next time you meet.

24

WHEN YOU FORGET THAT GOD NEVER FORGETS

Have you ever wondered if God has overlooked or forgotten you or your group?

Maybe you've had thoughts similar to the ones below:

If God cared He would do something.

God, can't you see what I am facing?

If God doesn't make something happen, I'm going under.

Do you know that many of the psalms portray the same type of struggle? Like many of the psalmists did, we too sometimes wrestle with the thought that God has forgotten us. In Psalm 77, the writer asked:

Will the Lord reject forever? Will He never show His favor again? Has His unfailing love vanished forever? Has His promise failed for all time? Has God forgotten to be merciful? Has He in anger withheld His compassion? **Psalm 77:7-9**

Many times throughout the book of Psalms the writers question God's awareness of their distress or situation. It's human nature, sinful nature, to consider that God is unconcerned about our present condition and future consequences. However, God is never absent or far away, despite what we believe.[13]

The writer of Psalm 77 goes on to recall the faithfulness of God in times past. This is helpful for followers of Christ because we too have a history with God. Because of this, a question can be raised that must be honestly answered:

"Based on the past, who is more forgetful, God or me?"

The next time you forget that God never forgets, remind yourself of the same truths that the psalmist recalled:

1. Remember where/what God has brought you from.

In verse 10 the psalmist confronts his questioning by remembering the delivering power of God:

Then I thought, "To this I will appeal: the years when the Most High stretched out His right hand.

I never want to forget how God has changed my life. Even though now, after all the years of serving the Lord, some of the things that held me captive in times past are very distant. I am determined to recall Gods deliverance from insecurities, addictions, and hopelessness.

Like the lyrics to this song reads:

"When I think about the Lord How He saved, how He raised me How He filled me with the Holy Ghost How He healed me to the uttermost When I think about the Lord How he picked me up turned me around How He set my feet on solid ground"

Being reminded of God's love inspires gratitude and praise which is key to pressing through a trying time or personal conflict.

2. Remember what God has done.

Next, the writer begins to recall all of the great works and miracles the Lord has done throughout his life:

---

[13] Psalm 46:1

I will remember the deeds of the Lord; yes, I will remember Your miracles of long ago. I will consider all Your works and meditate on all Your mighty deeds.

It is encouraging to know that God doesn't change.[14] This means we can take comfort in knowing that if God did great wonders on our behalf in the past, He will still do great things on our behalf in the present. He even knows our future![15]

Tough times will inevitably come to our life; it's a fact of life even as Christians, maybe more accurately, especially because of our faith.

In the midst of these times we have a choice: Forget the faithfulness of God, or remember that He never forgets us.

He is here for you.[16]

What trials has God delivered you or your group from? Take a minute to recall His faithfulness and write them down as a reminder.

---

[14] Hebrews 13:8
[15] Jeremiah 29:11
[16] Psalm 46:1

25

PRAYING WITH FAITH

> If the enemy gets the blame when things are bad should he also get the credit when things are good?
>
> Unknown

As a Christian and as a group leader learning to pray with faith is vital to our walk with God. I hope this final chapter encourages you to trust more in Jesus and to rely upon His faithfulness and power every day.

Here are three points to remember when your faith is tested:

1. Don't give the devil more credit than he deserves.

Is the enemy attacking more when things are difficult and less when things are easier or not as difficult?

If an enemy is a true enemy, there is constantly a battle. The devil's intentions are the same whether life seems comfortable or difficult to us. The problem may not be that you have opened a door for the devil to release trouble; it could be that you have not released God to intervene. More prayer will never be a bad thing.

Finally, my brethren, be strong in the Lord and in the power of His might. Put on the whole armor of God, that you may be able to stand against the wiles of the devil. For we do not wrestle against flesh and blood, but against principalities, against powers, against the rulers of the darkness of this age, against spiritual hosts of wickedness in the heavenly places. **Ephesians 6:10-12**

Therefore take up the whole armor of God, that you may be able to withstand in the evil day, and having done all, to stand. Stand therefore, having girded your waist with truth, having put on the breastplate of righteousness, and having shod your feet with the preparation of the gospel of peace; above all, taking the shield of faith with which you will be able to quench all the fiery darts of the wicked one. And take the helmet of salvation, and the sword of the Spirit, which is the word of God; praying always with all prayer and supplication in the Spirit, being watchful to this end with all perseverance and supplication for all the saints– **Ephesians 6:13-18**

Take a look at verse sixteen a little closer: *"above all, taking the shield of faith with which you will be able to quench all the fiery darts of the wicked one."*

Why the shield of faith above all?

- It takes faith to stand up for truth (vs. 14)
- It takes faith to believe we are the "righteousness of God through faith in Christ Jesus" (Romans 3:22)
- It takes faith to share the gospel (vs. 15)
- It takes faith to receive salvation. (vs. 17)
- It takes faith to believe the Word of God (vs. 17)
- The book of Hebrews emphasizes the importance of faith:

But without faith it is impossible to please Him, for he who comes to God must believe that He is, and that He is a rewarder of those who diligently seek Him. **Hebrews 11:6**

2. It's not our faith that extinguishes the fiery arrows but Who our faith is in.

Here are a few more things to consider concerning the shield:

A. The word shield is rooted in the word door.

The root word of shield is the same Greek word for door (or gate) in John 10:

I am the door. If anyone enters by Me, he will be saved, and will go in and out and find pasture. **John 10:9**

In prayer, who are you holding on to?

It's not that a person who uses the shield of faith is skillful in defeating the enemy but rather that they are holding up the Author and Finisher of their faith.

B. Who are you allowing to go before you?

Seeing then that we have a great High Priest who has passed through the heavens, Jesus the Son of God, let us hold fast our confession. For we do not have a High Priest who cannot sympathize with our weaknesses, but was in all points tempted as we are, yet without sin. Let us therefore come boldly to the throne of grace, that we may obtain mercy and find grace to help in time of need. **Hebrews 4:14-15**

And whatever you ask in My name, that I will do, that the Father may be glorified in the Son. If you ask anything in My name, I will do it. **John 14:13-14**

Jesus did not come to reduce the heat but to put out the fire.

...but whoever drinks of the water that I shall give him will never thirst. But the water that I shall give him will become in him a fountain of water springing up into everlasting life. **John 4:14**

It takes faith to ask God to provide for and bless our families. It takes faith to pray that our loved ones will experience salvation. It takes faith to ask God to have mercy on our country. This is not blind faith because it is faith in what God said He will do.

3. Faith is effective when it is based in God's Word

If Jesus is the essence of our faith than our prayers must be in agreement with what God has promised... Jesus will not break the Word of God.

But they have not all obeyed the gospel. For Isaiah says, "LORD, who has believed our report?" So then faith comes by hearing, and hearing by the word of God. But I say, have they not heard? Yes indeed: "Their sound has gone out to all the earth, and their words to the ends of the world. **Romans 10:16-18**

Faith comes by hearing God not by our ability to create faith. Faith comes not by us trying really hard, but by hearing.

So Jesus said to them, "Because of your unbelief; for assuredly, I say to you, if you have faith as a mustard seed, you will say to this mountain, 'Move from here to there,' and it will move; and nothing will be impossible for you. **Matthew 17:20**

It's not quantity but quality.

The quality of our faith will be diminished if it is not founded upon God's Word.
Without hearing the Word there is nothing for our faith to be established upon.

Which leads us to the question; if our faith is not founded upon God's Word, what is it based in? Hopes, desires, selfish motives, wants?

If we pray based on our desires rather than what we hear from God it will result in frustration.

Our prayers should lead our decisions. BUT, how often do our decisions lead our prayers?

Praying in faith will provide confidence for the decisions that you make. Praying in faith will provide strength for the battles that you face. Praying in faith will remind you Who your faith is in.

It's Been A Pleasure!

I hope you have enjoyed *Intentional Small Groups: A Complete Guide For Leaders* as much as I loved writing it. More than that, I hope you have received support, information, and guidance that will help you as you lead others in and towards Christian community and spiritual growth.

I would be so grateful to hear what you think of this guide. Would you be willing to send me your comments and feedback?

Send me a tweet: @EvanDoyletweets

Share on Facebook: theEvanDoyle

Email: evan@dailychristianhelp.com

However you choose it will be appreciated.

A CLOSING PRAYER

God, I ask you to equip those reading this with your ability, love, and strength to do what you ask them to do. Encourage them with Your peace and may their group experience community and grow spiritually in a greater way. Help them to live intentionally trusting and believing that *He who began a good work in you will carry it on to completion until the day of Christ Jesus* (Philippians 1:6).

EVAN DOYLE

Evan Doyle blogs frequently and has self-published a few books. He is also an associate pastor at a non-denominational church. He and his wife Tiffany are proud parents of three boys and live in southeast, Indiana.

BIBLIOGRAPHY

Scripture taken from The Message. Copyright ©1993, 1994, 1995, 1996, 2000, 2001, 2002. Used by permission of NavPress Publishing Group.

The Holy Bible, New International Version®, NIV® Copyright ©1973, 1978, 1984, 2011 by Biblica, Inc.® Used by permission. All rights reserved worldwide.

Greek Lexicon :: G2315 (KJV)." Blue Letter Bible. Sowing Circle. Web. 11 Mar, 2014. <http://www.blueletterbible.org/lang/lexicon/lexicon.cfm?Strongs=G2315&t=KJV>.

Merriam-Webster.com. 2014. http://www.merriam-webster.com (19 November 2014).

Ted Engstrom, *The Making of a Christian Leader*. Grand Rapids, MI: Zondervan, 2009

Guy P. Duffield and Nathaniel M. Van Cleave, *Foundations of Pentacostal Theology*. Los Angeles, CA: Foursquare Media, 2008

Leroy Eims, *The Lost Art Of Disciple Making*. Grand Rapids, MI: Zondervan, 1978

www.ingramcontent.com/pod-product-compliance
Lightning Source LLC
Chambersburg PA
CBHW070538030426
42337CB00016B/2257